PACKAGE DESIGN

daab

Who has not suffered at the hands of the cruel malfunction of packaging, been a victim of the breakable tabs of plastic cases or the so-called easy-to-open Tetra Paks and the child-proof caps that are so secure that even parents are unable to open them? Despite their sometimes negative connotations, why do consumers love packaging so much that it has turned into one of the conditions of commercial success? In effect, beyond its logistic functions of protection, packaging is not only designed to seduce the client and lead him/her to choose a particular product, rather than another similar one, but also to become the extension of the brand and the values that this embodies. The product aside, it is the materials enclosing it, their abundance or absence, colors, shapes and opening techniques that the consumer will approve. An arduous task for designers who, nevertheless, with the development of new materials, techniques and ecological awakening, are dedicated to making the practical beautiful and the beautiful practical, and seek new formulas of durability, adaptability and the economic and ecologic viability of packaging. The 116 examples chosen for *Package Design* take into consideration criteria such as function, optimizing transport and storage, the esthetic aspect and environmental-friendliness. Some of the projects presented are already commercialized, while others were created within the framework of a competition or a course. Regardless, all projects, be they minimalist or playful, have the same will to resolve the equation of the function of packaging versus the identity of the product it contains in the most original way possible.

Wer hat nicht schon einmal mit den qualvollen Problemen zu kämpfen gehabt, die durch *Packaging* entstehen können? Wer wurde nicht schon einmal zum Opfer von den kleinen Laschen an Plastikverpackungen die ständig kaputt gehen, von Tetrapacks mit so genannten „leicht-zu-öffnenden Verschlüssen", von Deckeln, die so sicher sind, dass sie weder Kinder noch Eltern aufbekommen? Wie ist es möglich, dass das *Packaging* von den Käufern so hoch geschätzt wird, sogar bis zu dem Punkt hin, sich in einen der Erfolgsfaktoren des Verkaufs eines Produktes verwandelt zu haben, nachdem es uns soviel Ärger bereitet hat? Tatsache ist, dass die Verpackung über ihre logistische Schutzfunktion hinaus nicht nur dazu dient, den Käufer zu überzeugen einen bestimmten Artikel anstatt eines anderen ähnlichen zu wählen, sondern sie verwandelt sich auch in die Erweiterung einer Marke und deren Werte. Es geht neben dem Produkt darum, dass die Materialien, die es umhüllen – üppig oder sparsam verwendet – ihre Farbe und Formen sowie die Öffnungsmechanismen auf den Käufer ansprechend wirken. Eine mühsame Arbeit für die Designer, die sich zwischen der Entwicklung neuer Materialien, Techniken und ökologischer Maßstäbe darum kümmern müssen, das Praktische in Schönes und das Schöne ins Praktische umzuwandeln, indem sie ständig neue Formeln suchen, die eine längere Haltbarkeit, Mehrwertigkeit und eine wirtschaftliche sowie ökologische Lebensfähigkeit garantieren. Die 116 Beispiele, die für *Package Design* ausgewählt wurden, berücksichtigen Kriterien wie Funktionalität, Optimierung im Hinblick auf Transport und Lagerung, die äußere Erscheinung und Umweltverträglichkeit. Einige der vorgestellten Projekte wurden schon vermarktet, während andere im Rahmen unterschiedlicher Wettbewerbe und Studien entstanden, alle jedoch, seien sie minimalistisch oder verspielt, haben eines gemeinsam: den Willen, auf möglichst originale Weise die Probleme zu lösen, die durch die Gegenüberstellung der Funktionalität einer Verpackung und der Identität eines Produktes entstehen können.

¿Quién no ha sufrido alguna vez con las crueles complicaciones derivadas del *packaging*? ¿Quién no ha sido víctima de lengüetas de retractilados plásticos que se rompen, de las aperturas autodenominadas fáciles de los Tetra Pak, de tapones tan seguros que ni los niños ni los padres son capaces de abrirlos? Después de habernos causado tantos disgustos, ¿cómo puede ser el *packaging* algo tan valorado por los consumidores hasta el punto de haberse convertido en uno de los factores del éxito comercial de un producto? El hecho es que, más allá de su función protectora, el embalaje está destinado no solamente a seducir al cliente y a forzarlo a escoger un artículo en lugar de otro similar, sino que se convierte a su vez en una prolongación de la marca y de los valores que ésta encarna. Además del producto, se trata también de que los materiales que lo rodean, su abundancia o su ausencia, sus colores, sus formas y sus técnicas de apertura atraigan al consumidor. Una ardua tarea para los diseñadores, quienes, entre el desarrollo de nuevos materiales, de técnicas y de medidas concienciadas ecológicamente, se afanan en convertir lo práctico en bello y lo bello en práctico, en busca de nuevas fórmulas que garanticen una mayor durabilidad, la polivalencia y la viabilidad económica y ecológica de los embalajes. Los 116 ejemplos seleccionados en *Package Design* tienen en cuenta criterios como la funcionalidad, la optimización del transporte y del almacenaje, la presencia estética y el respeto por el medio ambiente. Algunos de los proyectos presentados ya han sido comercializados, mientras que otros han sido concebidos en el marco de distintos concursos o estudios, si bien todos, ya sean minimalistas o lúdicos, tienen en común la misma voluntad de resolver de la manera más original posible el problema de conciliar la funcionalidad del embalaje con la identidad del producto que contiene.

Qui n'a pas déjà été victime de ces cruels disfonctionnement du packaging ? Victime des languettes des emballages plastiques qui se cassent, des ouvertures soi-disant faciles des tetra packs, des bouchons tellement sécurisés que ni les enfants ni les parents ne peuvent les ouvrir ? Après nous avoir causé tant de déboires, comment le packaging pouvait-il être cependant chéri par les consommateurs jusqu'à devenir l'une des conditions du succès commercial ? Le fait est que, au-delà de ses fonctions logistiques de protection, l'emballage est sensé non seulement séduire le client et le mener à choisir un article précis plutôt qu'un autre similaire, mais devenir aussi une extension de la marque et des valeurs que cette-ci incarne. Au-delà du produit, ce sont donc les matériaux qui l'entourent, leurs abondance ou absence, leurs couleurs, leurs formes, leurs techniques d'ouverture qui devront avoir raison du consommateur. Une tâche ardue pour les designers qui pourtant, entre développement de nouveaux matériaux, de techniques et prise de conscience écologique, se vouent à rendre beau le pratique et pratique le beau, cherchant de nouvelles formules à la durabilité, la polyvalence, la viabilité économique et écologique des emballages. Les 116 exemples sélectionnés dans *Package Design* prennent en compte les critères tels que la fonctionnalité, l'optimisation du transport et du stockage, l'esthétique et le respect de l'environnement. Certains des projets présentés sont déjà commercialisés, d'autres ont été crées dans le cadre de concours ou d'études, mais tous, qu'ils soient minimalistes ou ludiques, ont en commun la même volonté de résoudre le plus originalement possible l'équation de la fonctionnalité de l'emballage face à l'identité du produit qu'il contient.

Chi non ha sperimentato almeno una volta i perversi effetti del *packaging*? Chi non è stato vittima delle linguette del cellofan che si rompono, del così detto apri facile dei tetrapak, dei tappi così sicuri che né i bambini né i genitori sono capaci di aprirli? Dopo tutte le seccature che ci ha causato, come è possibile che il *packaging* sia così apprezzato dai consumatori tanto da diventare uno dei fattori che determinano il successo commerciale di un prodotto? Il fatto è che, al di là della funzione di protezione, la confezione non solo serve a sedurre il cliente e indirizzarlo verso la scelta di un articolo anziché di un altro, ma diviene a sua volta parte della marca e dei valori che essa rappresenta. Oltre al prodotto, è necessario che anche i materiali che lo avvolgono, la loro abbondanza o la loro assenza, il loro colore, la loro forma e i sistemi di apertura, attraggano il consumatore. Un compito difficile per i designer che, tra lo sviluppo di nuovi materiali e di nuove tecniche e l'applicazione di misure volte a proteggere l'ambiente, si affannano a trasformare ciò che è pratico in bello e ciò che è bello in pratico, in cerca di nuove formule che garantiscano una maggior durata, la polivalenza, la viabilità economica e la sostenibilità ecologica delle confezioni. I 116 esempi che compongono *Package Design* sono stati selezionati tenendo conto di criteri quali la funzionalità, l'ottimizzazione per il trasporto e lo stoccaggio, la presenza estetica e il rispetto per l'ambiente. Alcuni dei progetti che qui si presentano sono già in commercio, altri, invece, sono stati concepiti nel contesto di concorsi o studi, ma tutti, siano essi minimalisti o ludici, hanno in comune la stessa volontà di risolvere nel modo più originale possibile il problema di sposare la funzionalità della confezione con l'identità del prodotto che essa contiene.

AIRSIDE | LONDON
MUSIC PACKAGING
1 Lemonjelly Space Walk CD Single | 2004
2 Lemonjelly '64-'95 DVD Set | 2005
3 Lemonjelly Soft Rock / Rolled Oats
   Limited Edition 7" Vinyls | 2002-2003

ORIGINAL SOURCE

MINT AND TEA TREE SHOWER

PACKED WITH ESSENTIAL OILS

FULLER, THICKER LOOKING HAIR

NEW

ORIGINAL SOURCE

TANGERINE AND BERGAMOT

BODY BOOSTING SHAMPOO

FOR FINE / LIFELESS HAIR

ORIGINAL SOURCE

LAVENDER AND TEA TREE

DEEP SOAK BATH FOAM

PACKED WITH NATURAL ESSENTIAL OILS
TOTALLY REFRESHING

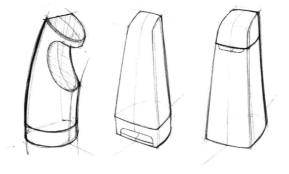

SHOK™

AVEC ARÔME DE GUARANA,
UNE SOURCE NATURELLE DE CAFÉINE†

Labatt
BLEUE®
Pilsener

BOISSON DE MALT
6,9% alc./vol. 250 mL

BAG.DISSENY | BARCELONA
T-SHIRT PACK CLIPPACK
Any del Disseny | 2003

ESSO
ULTRA

TURBO
DIESEL
10W-40

MOTOR
OIL

Esso

BARSKIDESIGN | FRANKFURT AM MAIN

1 ESSO ULTRA
Exxon Mobile | 2005

2 FÜRSTENBERG
Fürstenberg | 1999

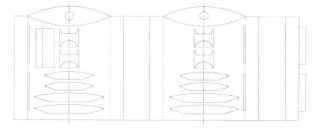

BEATRIZ PÉREZ, CLARA BURGUILLO | BARCELONA
GINA SCOOTER
Escola Massana / Pro Carton Packaging Seminar | 2006

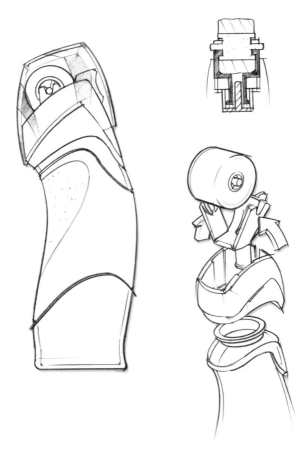

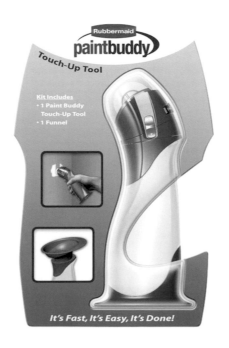

BIG-GAME | LAUSANNE
BOX
BIG-GAME | 2004

In folded aluminum. Still a box, no longer
makeshift as a seat.

BLOOM | LONDON
23 MIXER
Diageo | 2004

3 Color-coded flavors, stackable bottles.

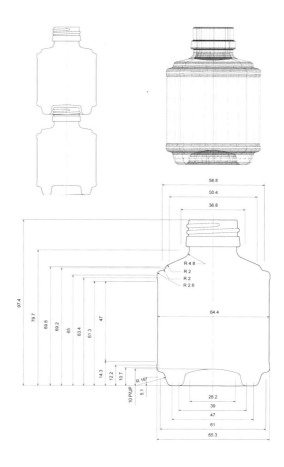

BRANDES EN MEURS INDUSTRIAL DESIGN | UTRECHT

1 DREMEL TOOL KIT
  Dremel | 2004

2 SKIL DRILL GUN
  Skil Europe | 2004

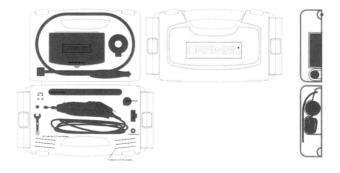

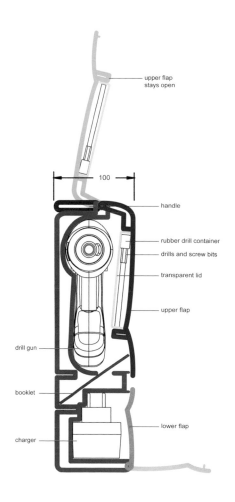

upper flap
stays open

100

handle

rubber drill container

drills and screw bits

transparent lid

upper flap

drill gun

booklet

lower flap

charger

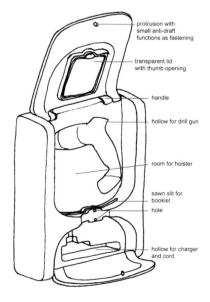

protrusion with
small anti-draft
functions as fastening

transparent lid
with thumb opening

handle

hollow for drill gun

room for holster

sawn slit for
booklet

hole

hollow for charger
and cord

for dreamers, optimists and do-gooders

SCHRŒDER

skim

SKIM
MILK
VITAMINS A & D
FAT FREE   GRADE A

HALF GALLON (1 89 L)

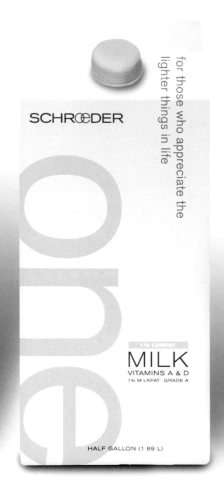

for those who appreciate the lighter things in life

SCHRŒDER

one

1% LOWFAT
MILK
VITAMINS A & D
1% M LKFAT   GRADE A

HALF GALLON (1 89 L)

SCHROEDER

two

for growing kids, purists or those
trying to recapture their childhood

2% REDUCED FAT

MILK
VITAMINS A & D
2% MILKFAT GRADE A

HALF GALLON (1 89 L)

SCHROEDER

two

for growing kids, purists or those
trying to recapture their childhood

2% REDUCED FAT

MILK
VITAMINS A & D
2% M LKFAT GRADE A

GALLON (3.78 L)

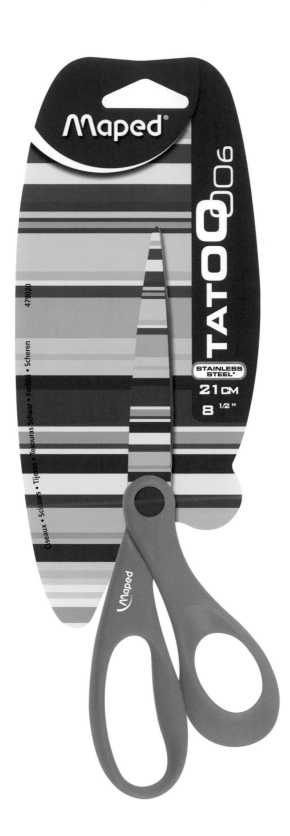

CARACAS | LYON/VILLEURBANNE
SCISSORS TATTOO PACKAGE
Maped | 2005

CATALINA HERMIDA, ELISE LAMMER | BARCELONA
ADVENTURE FIRST AID KIT
Escola Massana / Pro Carton Packaging Seminar | 2003

DONUT TAPE DISPENSER
Dalton Packaging | 2005

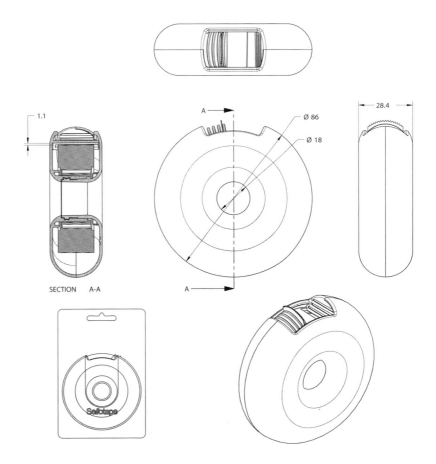

1.1

SECTION   A-A

A

Ø 86

Ø 18

A

28.4

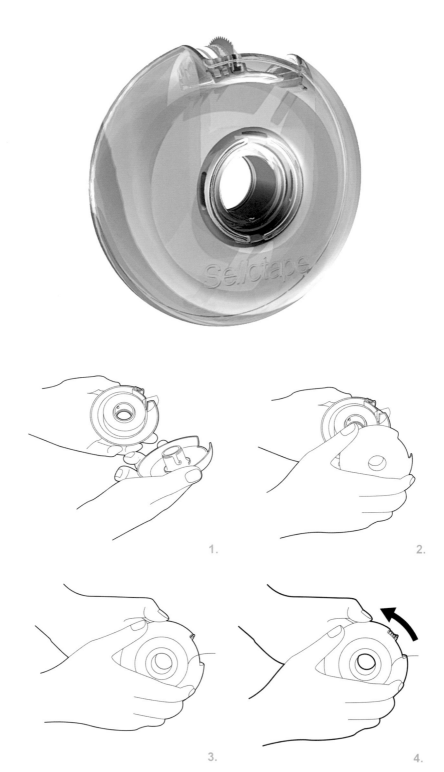

1.

2.

3.

4.

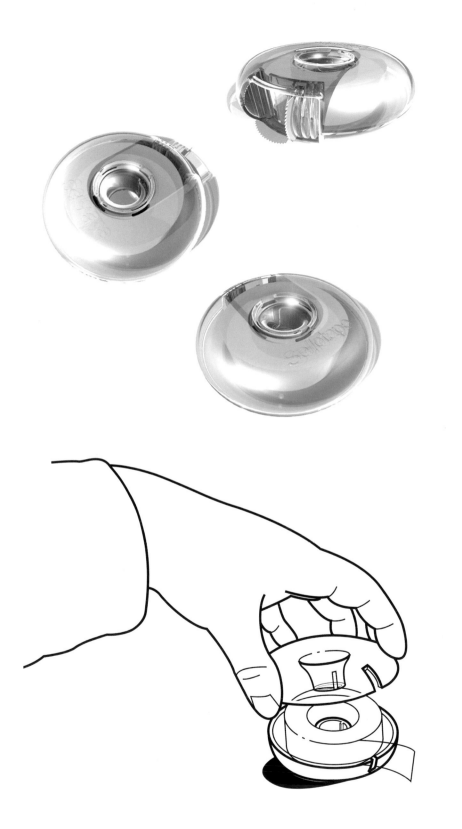

COCKTAILS BY

jenn™

KEY LIME MARTINI

premium
vodka cocktail

4-100 ML BOTTLES

COCKTAILS BY

jenn™

KEY LIME

vodka with natural flavors
certified color

17% ALC. BY VOL.

COCKTAILS BY JENN | NEW YORK
BOTTLES AND 4-PACK
Cocktails by Jenn | 2004

AROMATIC BODY MILK

木

EQUILIR

土

EQUILIR

AROMATIC BODY WASH

COMFORTABLE BODY VEIL

宙   EQUILIR

LISTEN TO YOUR NOSE   IT SENSES W

CURIOSITY | TOKYO

1 EQUILIR COSMETICS
  Kanebo Cosmetics | 2002

2 PARFUM CURIOSITY
  Curiosity | 2002

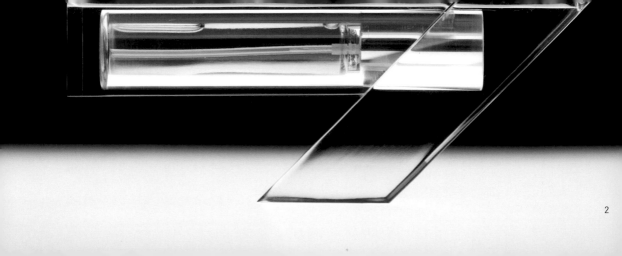

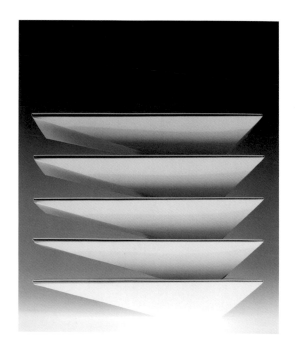

DANIEL RACAMIER | PRINGY

1 BOX SCISSORS CRÉA CUT
  Maped | 2005

2 FLEXBOX COLOR'PEPS
  Maped | 2005

3 PROTECT BOX COLOR'PEPS
  Maped | 2004

DANIEL RACAMIER & FRANÇOIS AZNAR FOR GALB | PRINGY
RUBBER ZENOA
Maped | 2001

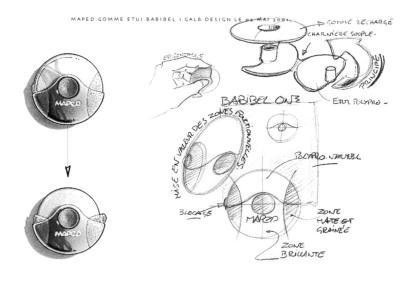

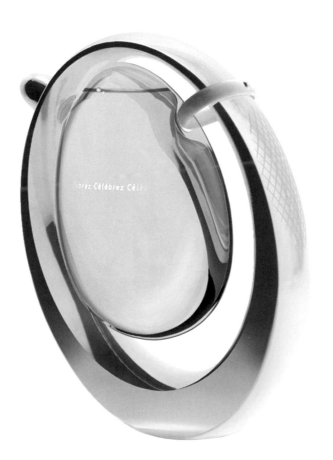

DCA DESIGN INTERNATIONAL | WARWICK

1 CÉLÉBREZ BOTTLE
DCA Design International | 2005
Platinum carafe emphasizes value of water
contained in refillable pouch.

2 DRINK MAINTAIN PACKAGE
DCA Design International | 2005
Minute-made pouch: describes and protects the
customized drink's nutrient value.

3 E MILK BOTTLE
DCA Design International | 2004
Reusable, customizable. Eco-friendly paper,
battery-fuelled digital display.

4 FRUIT BLAST
DCA Design International | 2005
Customizable, healthy. A choice of fruit gel-filled
caps flavor the drink.

5 REWARD VIAL
DCA Design International | 2005
Releases aroma when warmed by the hand,
decorated
with heat-sensitive ink.

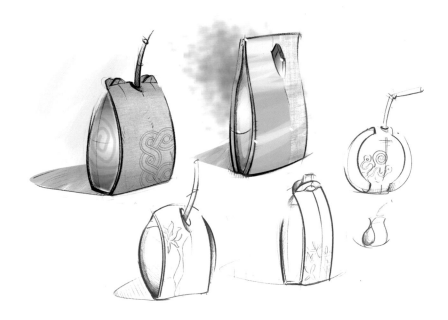

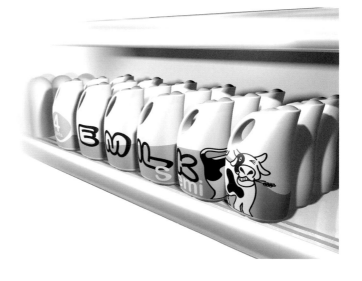

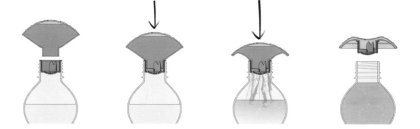

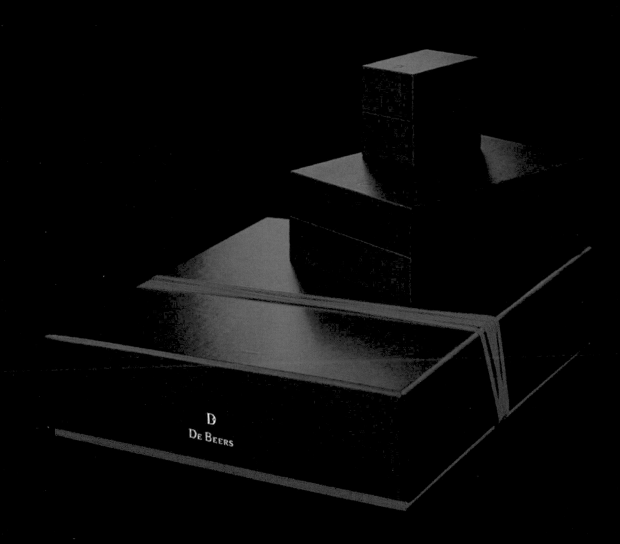

DEW GIBBONS, SEBASTIAN BERGNE | LONDON, BOLOGNA
DE BEERS JEWELRY PACKAGE
De Beers LV | 2002

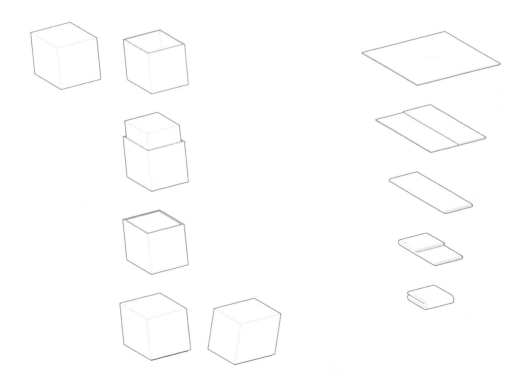

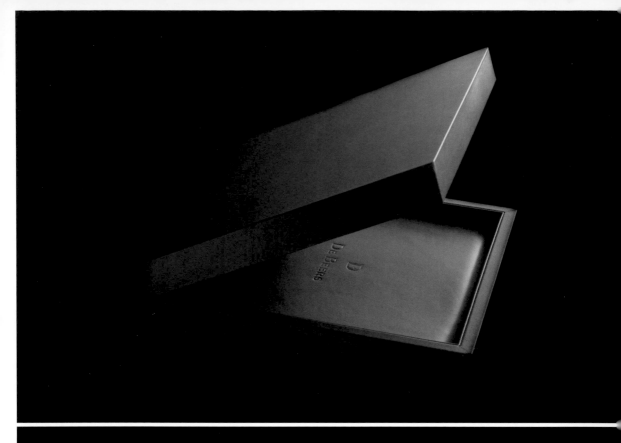

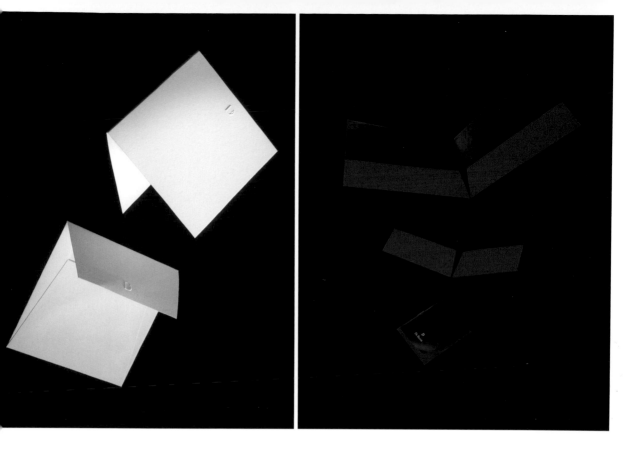

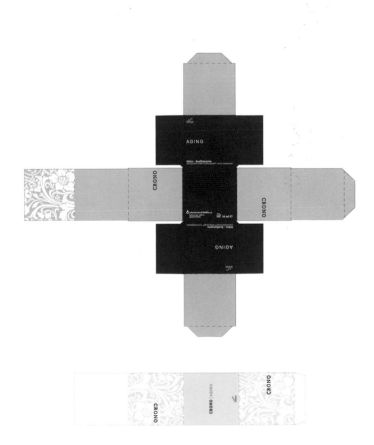

FORM US WITH LOVE | KALMAR
BENDABLE INTERIOR OBJECTS
Eurosteel | 2005

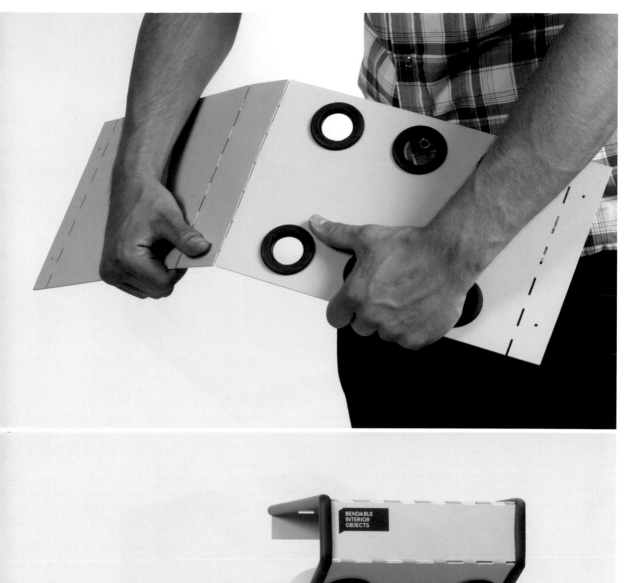

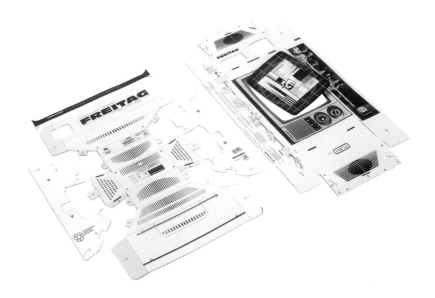

GERARD MOLINÉ FOR AZUAMOLINE.COM | BARCELONA
URNA BIOS
C.I.R.E. | 2000

Biodegradable funerary urn with seed.
Once planted, a tree grows from the ashes.

GILLES CENAZANDOTTI FOR SARTORIA COMUNICAZIONE | SAINT OUEN
LIMITED EDITION DEFUMO DVD PACKAGE
Defumo | 2002

GROOVISIONS | TOKYO
100% CHOCOLATE CAFE PACKAGING
Meiji Seika Kaisha | 2004

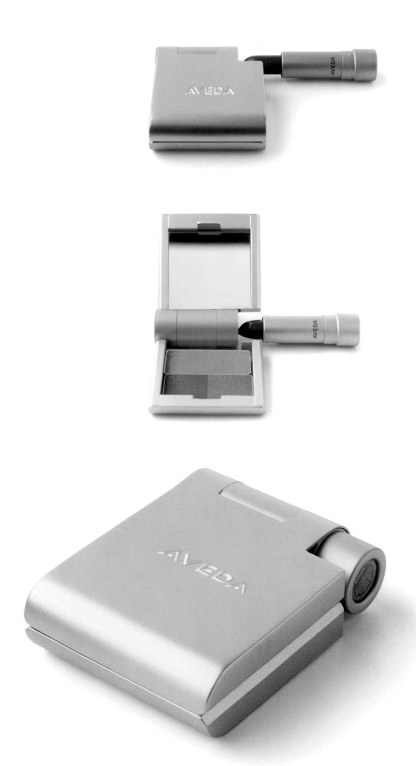

HARRY ALLEN & ASSOCIATES | NEW YORK

1 ESSENTIALS COMPACT
  Aveda | 2004

2 UKURU LIP PIGMENT
  Aveda | 2003
  Refillable lipstick case.

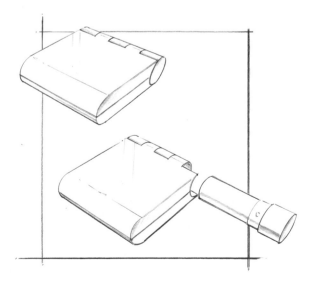

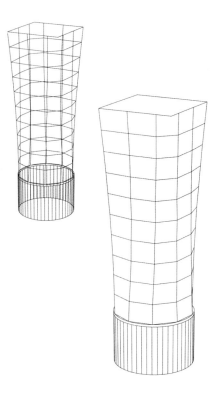

ICON DEVELOPMENT GROUP | TORRANCE
TRESDON WINE RACK
FRANCIS FORD COPPOLA WINERY | 2006

Carrying case transforms into expandable storage rack.

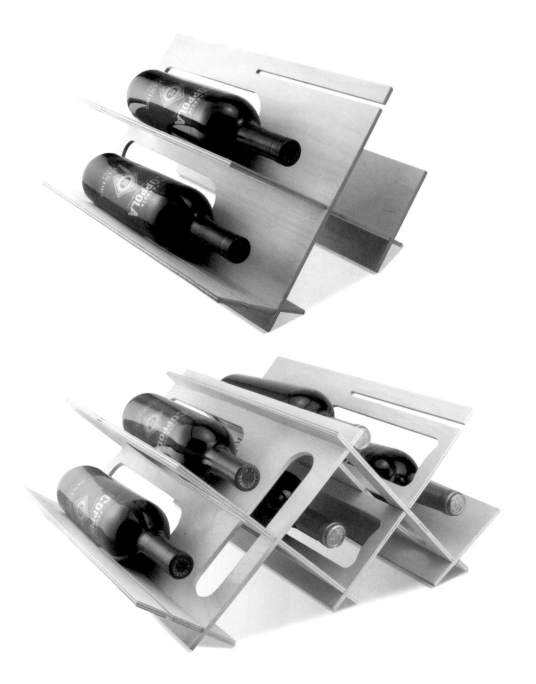

IDEO | LONDON
NATUREWORKS "PLA" BIO-PLASTIC CONCEPTS
IDEO | 2006

Perfume bottle and energy drink bottles made of PLA,
a corn-derivated plastic.

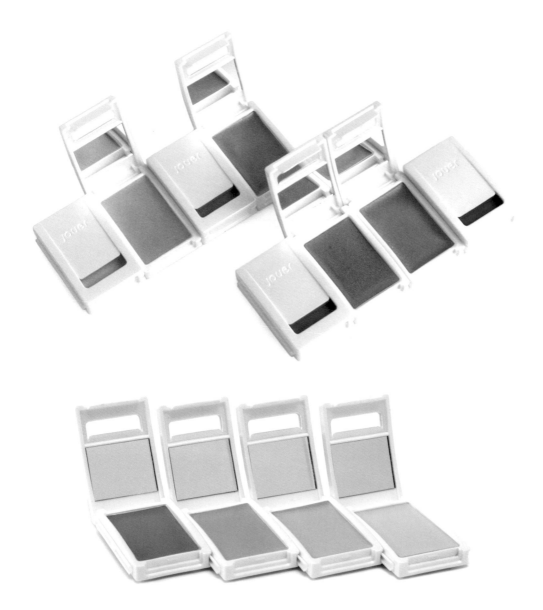

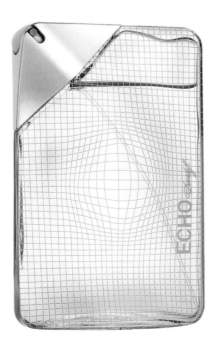
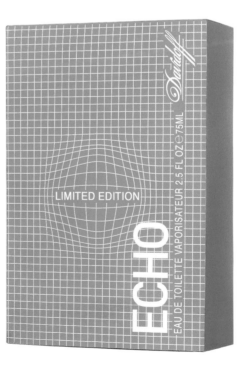

KARIM RASHID | NEW YORK

1 ECHO BY DAVIDOFF
  Davidoff | 2004

2 ISSEY MIYAKE'S FATHER'S DAY KIT
  Issey Miyake | 2002

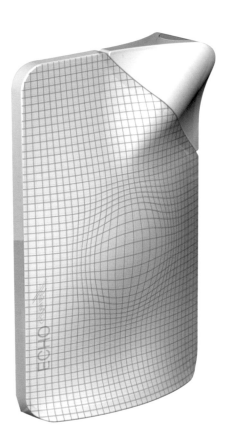
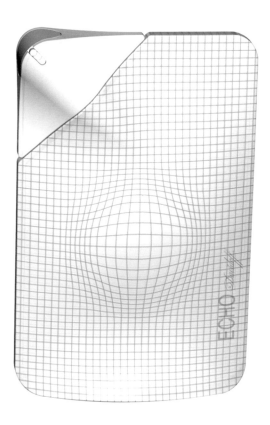

KEJADONIA DESIGN & COMMUNICATIE | SCHIPHOL-OOST
ROYAL CLUB BOTTLES
Vrumona | 2004

DIARY

TIME OF REBIRTH
DEBUT ALBUM BY THE OBSERVATORY

KINETIC SINGAPORE | SINGAPORE
THE OBSERVATORY CD COVER
The Observatory | 2004

~~A No~~
~~Observant~~
~~Observatory Isle~~
~~Observation~~
The Observatory *
~~The Obscure~~
~~Lifelong~~

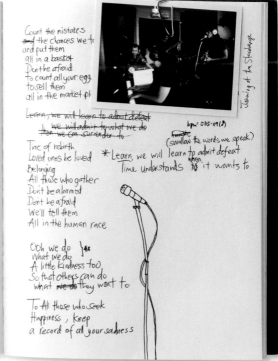

Listening at the Soundstage

Count the mistakes
~~and~~ the chances we to
and put them
all in a basket
Dont be afraid
to count all your eggs
to sell them
all in the market pl

~~Learn, we will learn to admit defeat~~
~~then~~ We will admit to what we do
we can surrender to

bpm: 115-119 (?)
(swallow the words we speak)

Time of rebirth
Loved ones be loved
Belonging
All those who gather
Dont be alarmed
Dont be afraid
We'll tell them
All in the human race

* Learn, we will learn to admit defeat
Time understands when it wants to

Ooh we do |4x
What we do
A little kindness too
So that others can do
what ~~we do~~ they want to

To All those who ~~seek~~
Happiness , keep
a record of all your sadness

(left page)

[tally marks]

~~time~~ time of Rebirth

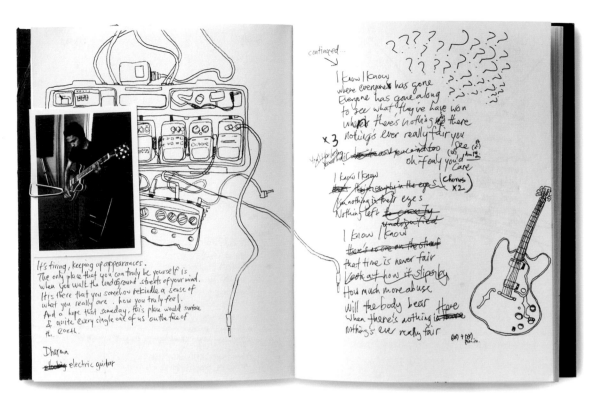

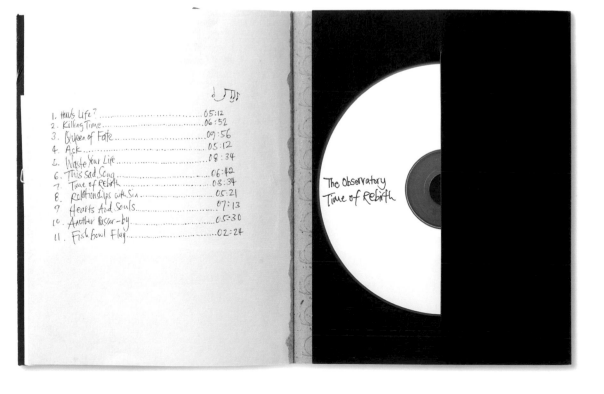

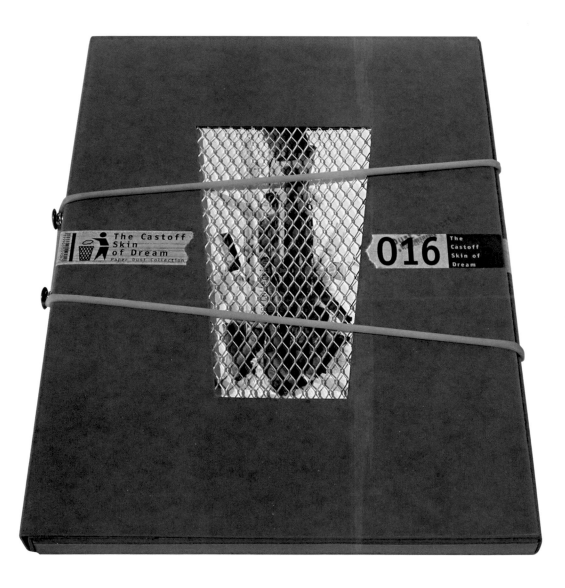

KOKOKUMARU | OSAKA

1 DUST BOOK
Takeo Paper | 1999

2 KEKKAI BOOK
Oji Paper | 2001

3 ROBOCUP 2005 OSAKA
RoboCup 2005 Osaka Committee | 2005

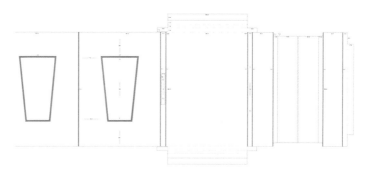

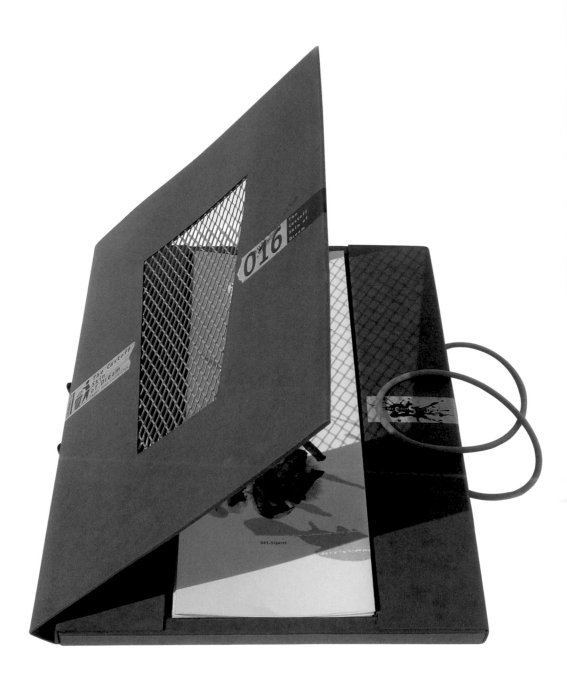

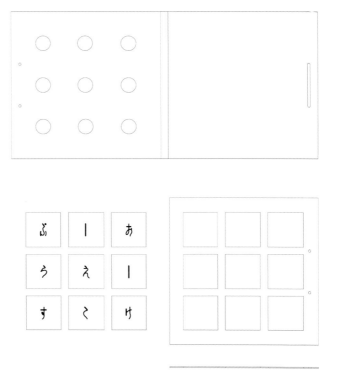

KE XK AI -3

Even without walls, symbolism that consciouslysets space apart divides space effectively. This is called *KEKKAI*. Although we cannot touch the boundary, the world of consciousness changes radically as we move in and out of *KEKKAI*.

KE XK AI -2

Even without walls, symbolism that consciouslysets space apart divides space effectively. This is called *KEKKAI*. Although we cannot touch the boundary, the world of consciousness changes radically as we move in and out of *KEKKAI*.

KE XK AI -1

Even without walls, symbolism that consciouslysets space apart divides space effectively. This is called *KEKKAI*. Although we cannot touch the boundary, the world of consciousness changes radically as we move in and out of *KEKKAI*.

3

press kit

RoboCup
2005
OSAKA

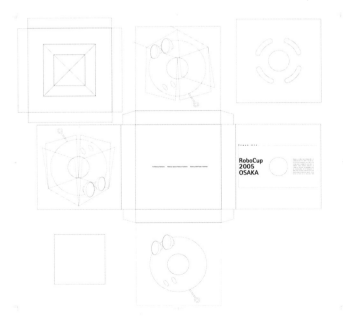

RoboCup
2005
OSAKA

LANDOR ASSOCIATES, YANNICK LENORMAND | LONDON
EVIAN ORIGINE
Danone | 2005

LAURA MILLÁN | BARCELONA

1 COSMETIC PACKAGING VIJUVI
  El envase reversible | 2006

2 YOGOY
  El envase reversible | 2006

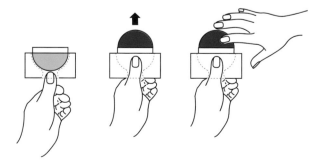

2

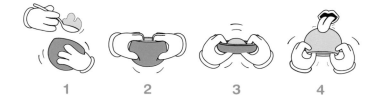

1   2   3   4

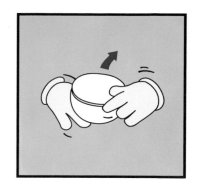

LAURA NOGALEDO, RUT ROVIRA | BARCELONA
GALILEO GALILEI SECTOR
Escola Massana / Pro Carton Packaging Seminar | 2006

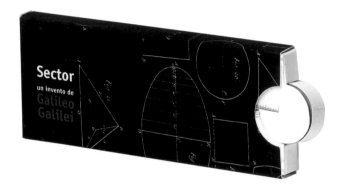

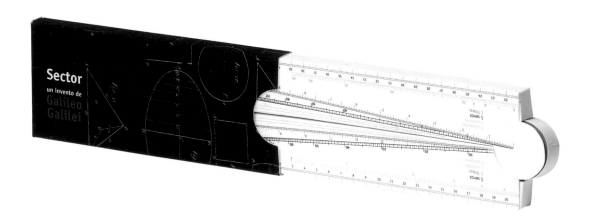

LISTON + PLATON | SURRY HILLS
KEVIN MURPHY HAIR CARE PRODUCTS
Kevin Murphy | 2004

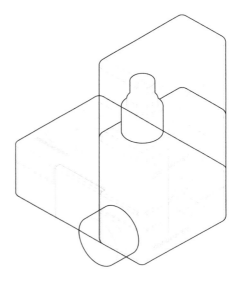

ANTI.GRAVITY
KEVIN.MURPHY
150ml 5.1fl.oz e

ANTI.GRAVITY is a multipurpose lotion that acts as a volumiser and gentle texturizer. Apply to wet hair and dry in for a look that defies gravity. Certified Organic Lavender gives the hair life and shine. This product may also be used to define your style by applying a small amount after the hair has been dried. ANTI.GRAVITY is weightless and contains no oil. Suits all hair types in need of volume and definition, particularly fine hair or straighter styles. Great for chemically straightened hair.

INGREDIENTS: Lavender Hydrosol, PVP Copolymer, PVP/DMAPA Acrylates Copolymer, Hydroxyethyl Acrylate/ Sodium Acryloyldimethyl Taurate Copolymer, Squalane (Vegetable), Polysorbate 60, Polysorbate 20, Honey Extract Apis mellifera, Citrus Seed Extract, Essential Oil of Ho Leaf Cinnamomum camphora, CI 42090, CI 45430, CI 16255.

L'Attitude Global Holdings Pty Ltd.
P.O. BOX 7068 St Kilda Road, Melbourne 8004, Australia.
Product of Australia. www.kevinmurphy.com.au

KEVIN.MURPHY
250ml

KEVIN.MURPHY
250ml

MAXI.WASH
KEVIN.MURPHY
250ml 8.4fl.oz e

A deep shampoo to strip unwanted product residue and excess oil that can build up in your hair. Tropical fruit acids (AHA) and anti pollution agents deeply cleanse the hair. Sage Extracts dissolve the fats and oils. A herbal blend of Lime, Mint and Eucalyptus remove excess oil and stimulate sluggish scalps. Apply to wet hair and gently massage into hair and scalp, rinse and repeat. Do not scrub your scalp.

INGREDIENTS: Aqueous Extract of Sage Salvia officinalis, Magnesium Laureth Sulfate, Sodium Cleth Sulfate, Cocobetaine, Decyl Glucoside, Olive Oil Esters Olea europaea, Alpha Hydroxy Fruit Acids of Pineapple & Papaya & Citrus, Glyceryl Laurate, PEG-120 Methyl Glucose Dioleate, Polysorbate 20, Citrus Seed Extract, Sage Leaf Salvia officinalis, Essential Oil of Lime West Indian Citrus aurantifolia, Essential Oil of Grapefruit Pink Citrus paradisi, Essential Oil of Ylang Ylang Complete Cananga odorata, Essential Oil of White Camphor Cinnamomum camphora, Essential Oil of Pacific Island Niaouli Melaleuca quinquenervia, Essential Oil of Sage Salvia officinalis, Menthol Crystals.

L'Attitude Global Holdings Pty Ltd.
P.O. BOX 7068 St Kilda Road, Melbourne 8004, Australia.
Product of Australia. www.kevinmurphy.com.au

BORN.AGAIN
KEVIN.MURPHY
150ml 5.1fl.oz e

Put suffering hair to an end. This conditioning treatment will replenish tortured hair. Chemically damaged hair is 'Born Again'. Conditioning agents derived from Olive Leaf, Shea Butter, Omega 3 & Omega 6 soften, repair and moisturise. Apply to wash. Leave in hair and massage through the hair and scalp. Leave in for a minimum of two minutes the longer the product is left in the deeper the penetration.

INGREDIENTS: Aqueous Extract of Bamboo Bambusa arundinacea, Hydrolyzed Silk Protein, Cetrimonium Chloride, Behentrimonium Methosulfate, Emulsifying Wax, Omega 3 & Omega 6, Olive Leaf Extract, Oleic acid Olea europaea.

GRITTY.BUSINESS
Strong Hold. Moulding Clay

K

KEVIN.MURPHY
150ml

STICKY.BUSINESS
KEVIN.MURPHY
130ml 4.4fl.oz ℮

9 332747 000069

STICKY.BUSINESS is a matte finish texturizer, which simultaneously holds
and separates the hair. Baronia and Tangerine essences give the hair shine and
holding power, creating a deliberately dishevelled look. The products moisture
content controls frizz without weighing down

EASY.RIDER
Anti Frizz Creme. Flexible Hold

to dry or damp
hair and mould in to ... ut in water.

...mer, Cetearyl Alcohol
... Purified Lanolin Oil,
...: Grapefruit Pink
...nia megastigma,

12M

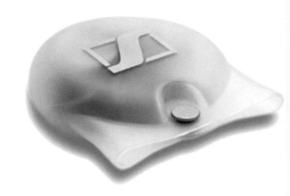

LONDONBERLIN | LONDON, BERLIN
TRANSPORT, STYLE AND CHROME BOX FOR EARPHONE SPORT
Sennheiser | 2006

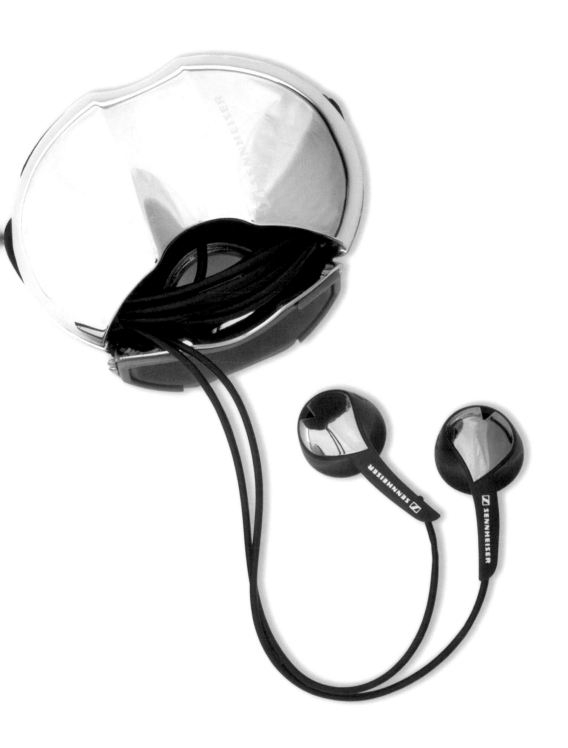

MARC ATLAN DESIGN | VENICE (CA)
COMME DES GARÇONS FRAGRANCES COLLECTION
Comme des Garçons | 1993-2000

COMME des GARÇONS
Essence pour le Bain
Bath Essence
COMME des GARÇONS
50ml 1,7fl.oz. Product of France
Comme des Garçons Parfum S.A. Paris
COMME des GARÇONS
ODEUR 53 EAU DE TOILETTE
COMME DES GARÇONS PARFUM S.A. 16 PLACE VENDÔME 75001 PARIS. INGREDIENTS: ALCOHOL DENAT (65% VOL.), AQUA, PARFUM. CONTENTS: SD ALCOHOL 39-C (65% VOL.), WATER, FRAGRANCE. CET ARTICLE NE PEUT ÊTRE VENDU QUE PAR LES DÉPOSITAIRES AGRÉES COMME DES GARÇONS. PRODUCT OF FRANCE.
COMME des GARÇONS
200 ML. 6.8FL.OZ.
VAPORISATEUR NATURAL SPRAY
COMME des GARÇONS
COMME des GARÇONS
eau de cologne
ODEUR 53
LIQUID SOAP
SAVON LIQUIDE
COMME DES GARÇONS PARFUM S.A. 16 PLACE VENDÔME 75001 PARIS. CET ARTICLE NE PEUT ÊTRE VENDU QUE PAR LES DÉPOSITAIRES AGRÉES COMME DES GARÇONS. PRODUCT OF FRANCE.
150 ML. 5.07 FL.OZ.
COMME des GARÇONS
COMME des GARÇONS
CANDLE BOUGIE
COMME des GARÇONS
100ml 3.4fl.oz. Eau de Parfum Product of France
Comme des Garçons Parfum S.A. Paris
50ml 1.7fl.oz.
COMME des GARÇONS white
EAU DE TOILETTE
COMME DES GARÇONS PARFUM S.A. PARIS.
Product of France
CANDLE BOUGIE
COMME des GARÇONS
jewel
COMME des GARÇONS
50ml 1.7fl.oz. Eau de Parfum
PARFUMS
PARFUMS
COMME des GARÇONS
ODEUR 53
EAU DE TOILETTE
COMME des GARÇONS
COMME des GARÇONS
jewel
COMME des GARÇONS
50ml 1.7fl.oz. Eau de Parfum
COMME des GARÇONS

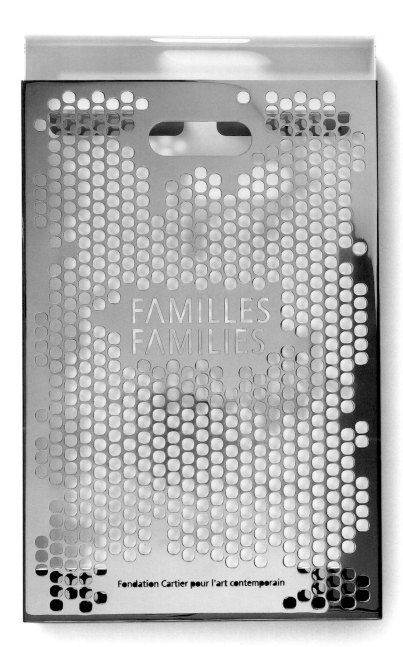

FAMILLES
FAMILIES

Fondation Cartier pour l'art contemporain

1

MATHIEU LEHANNEUR | PARIS

1 FAMILLES-FAMILIES
  Fondation Cartier pour l'art contemporain | 2005

2 THERAPEUTIC OBJECTS
  MoMA Permanent Collection | 2001
  1 The dose of medication is integrated into a
  paper handkerchief.
  2 Gradually dissolves by effervescence, its action
  uncovering silent symptoms.
  3 This medication peels like an onion, one layer
  per day.
  4 Between doses, the box inflates to indicate
  necessity of next take.

1

4

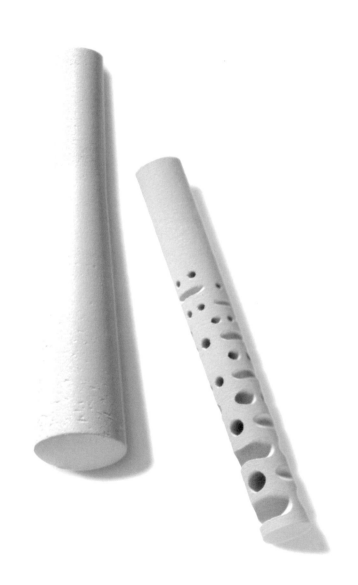

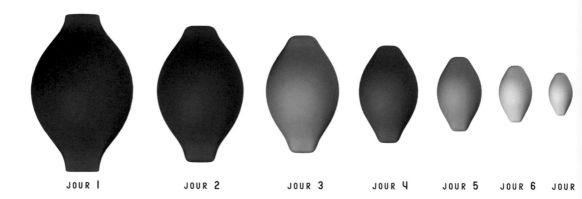

JOUR 1   JOUR 2   JOUR 3   JOUR 4   JOUR 5   JOUR 6   JOUR

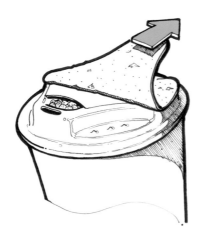

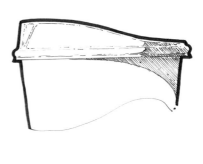

MIHOKO HACHIUMA FOR OFFICE M | KOCHI
"IMO KEMPI" PACKAGING
Shibuya Foods | 2005

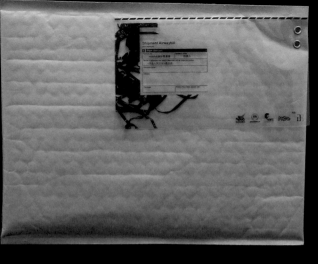

MILKXHAKE | KENNEDY TOWN
MOTCLUB 903
Hong Kong Commercial Radio | 2005

MORERA DESIGN | BARCELONA

1 VV MAN
  Perfumes y Diseño | 2004

2 VV WOMAN
  Perfumes y Diseño | 2002

NO PICNIC | STOCKHOLM

1 ANKLE AND ELBOW REHBAND SUPPORTS
Otto Bock Scandinavia | 2005

2 SPACE FOOD PACKAGING
NASA / ESA | 2000

3 SPORT UNDERWEAR PACKAGING
Houdini Sportswear | 2004

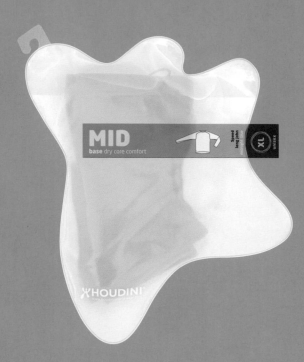

MID base dry core comfort · Speed long john · **XL** · unisex

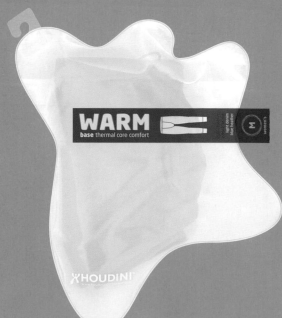

WARM base thermal core comfort · light denim blue heather · **M** · women's

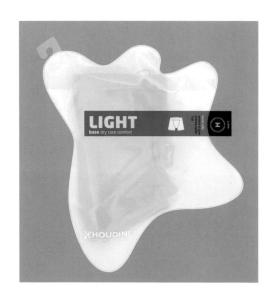

OLIVIER MARRACHE FOR DESIGNUM TREMENS | TOULOUSE
GLASS
Designum Tremens | 2004

A new take on the traditional optical phenomenon.

moulded glass

PAPERMINT DESIGN | COPENHAGEN
THE BEAUTIFUL SWAN
De Danske Spritfabrikker | 2004

PARKER WILLIAMS | LONDON
DISNEY DOUGH
Disney | 2005

2

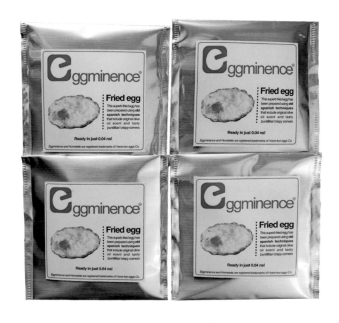

PURE EQUATOR | NOTTINGHAM
LABEL M HAIRCARE LINE
Toni & Guy | 2006

RADI DESIGNERS | PARIS
MARLBORO MATCHES
Philip Morris | 2003

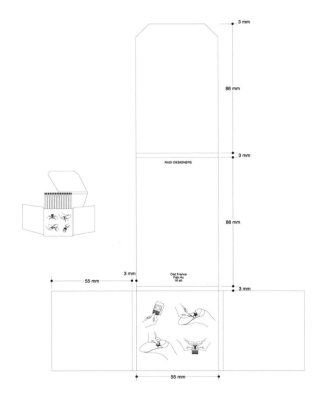

RDYA | BUENOS AIRES

1 RDYA PROMOTIONAL PACKAGING
   RDYA | 2004-2005

2 VAJA
   Vaja | 2006

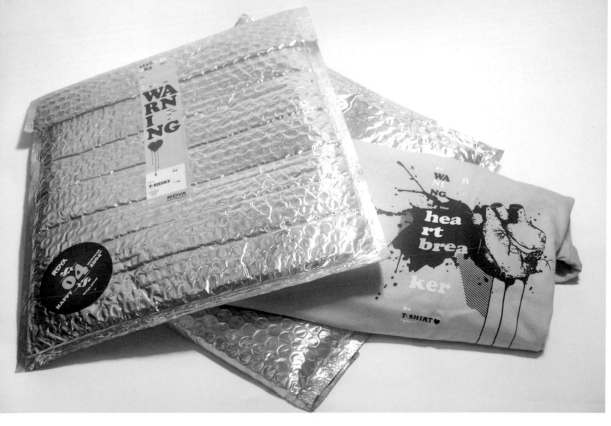

cuidado con
"el cactus"

RICARDO MANRIQUE, ANDER SOLANO | BARCELONA
PACKAGING FOR CACTUS
Escola Massana / Pro Carton Packaging Seminar | 2006

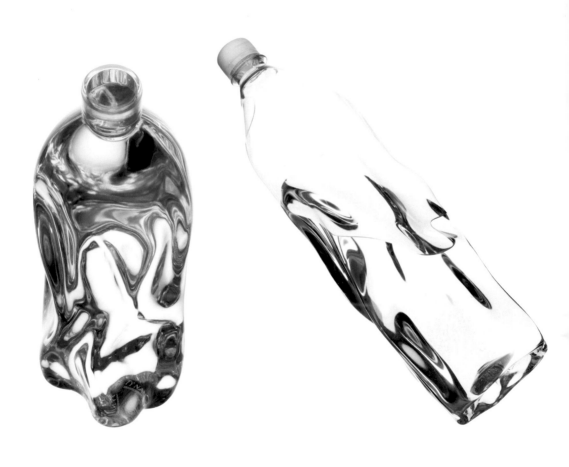

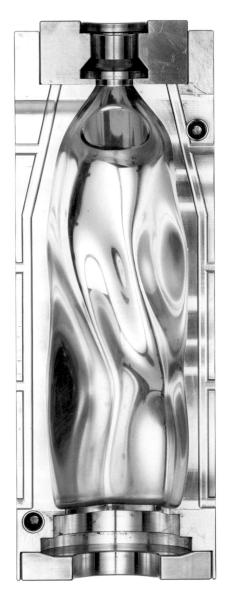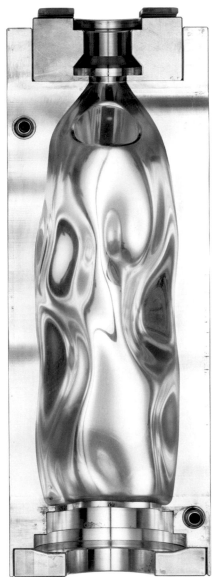

SKELETON KEY

1

SAGMEISTER | NEW YORK

1 SKELETON KEY CD
Motel Records | 1997

2 THE VANITY ALLEGORY
Deutsche Bank, Solmon R. Guggenheim Foundation | 2005

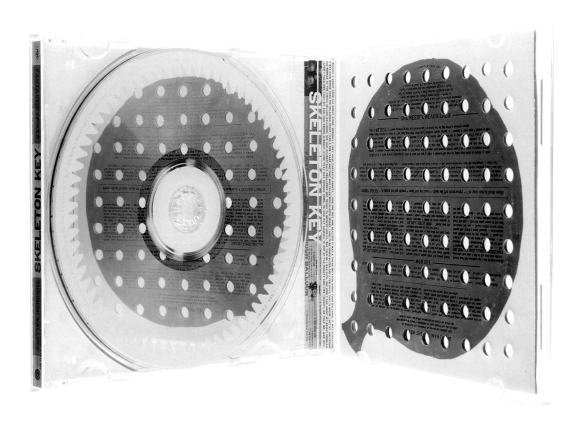

BOIS VERT

PARFUM
DE MAISON

Lafayette
MAISON

PARFUM
DE MAISON

Lafayette
MAISON

SAGUEZ AND PARTNERS | SAINT-OUEN
LAFAYETTE MAISON RANGE
Lafayette Maison | 2004

6 VERRES BALLON 25cl

ALL NATURAL
GOOD BUDDY™

CASTOR & POLLUX
PAW ✕ MADE
"WE MAKE STUFF WE LIKE"

C&P

COOKIES

THERE'S NO SUCH THING
AS A BAD DOG

Dog treats made with real peanut butter

PEANUT BUTTER

NET WT. 16 OZ. (454g)

A good day for a dog is a good day for all.

1

SANDSTROM DESIGN | PORTLAND (OR)

1 CASTOR & POLLUX RANGE OF PRODUCTS
Castor & Pollux | 2000
Designed by imaginary animals, for Animals.

2 GDIAPERS PACKAGING
gDiapers | 2005
Blue banner detaches and doubles as
a user guide.

g

gdiapers

S

S
6-13 lbs
3-6 kgs

flushable diaper starter kit

500 years is a long time.

putting on a gDiaper

flushing the flushable.

gDiaper tips.

gdiapers

inquiring minds want to know.

1. Why is flushing good?
2. Where can I learn more about flushing, pressure and plumbing?
3. Who started gDiapers?
4. What does the 'g' stand for?
5. Where can I get more gDiapers?

a guide to making this guide.
Remove end tabs and accordion fold.

stephanemarais | **Rouge Envoûtant**
Rouge à Lèvres
Liquide
Liquid Lip Color

℮ 6ml NET WT. .2OZ.

SERGIO CALATRONI ART ROOM | MILAN
STEPHANE MARAIS COSMETICS
Stephane Marais | 2001

TANK TROMSØ | TROMSØ
SMRPRTY BEER BOTTLE
Macks Ølbryggeri | 2004

Named after text message abbreviation
for summer party.

THE PARTNERS | LONDON

1 STANLEY HONEY
Charles Stanley | 2005
Reuse this pot to continue
the cycle: flowers, bee, honey.

2 STELLA MCCARTNEY BAGS
Stella McCartney | 2005
Each dot is a laser cut-out
through paper or ribbon.

STANLEY HONEY
BEES ARE HARD WORKING CREATURES
COLLECTING NECTAR FROM ALL OVER CLAPHAM.
REUSE THIS POT
TO GROW MORE FLOWERS AND
KEEP OUR BEES BUSY!

STANLEY HONEY
BEES ARE HARD WORKING CREATURES
COLLECTING NECTAR FROM ALL OVER CLAPHAM.
REUSE THIS POT
TO GROW MORE FLOWERS AND
KEEP OUR BEES BUSY!

TURNSTYLE | SEATTLE

1 DRY SODA BOTTLES
Dry Soda | 2005

2 TEAGUE MAILER
Teague | 2005

THIS BOX IS 100% RECYCLABLE

TEAGUE

FROM:

TEAGUE
2727 WESTERN AVENUE
NUMBER 200
SEATTLE, WA 98121

TO:

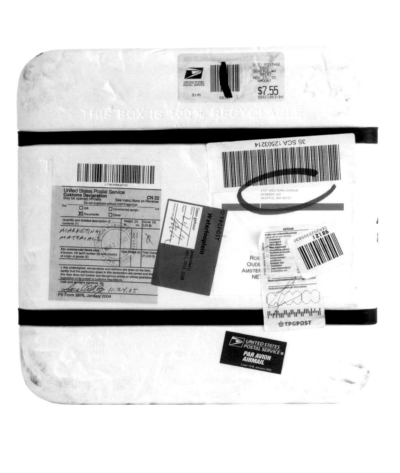

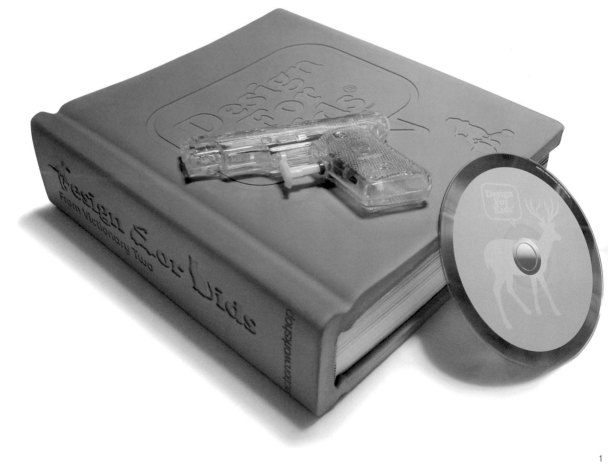

VICTION:ARY | NORTH POINT

1 BOOK DESIGN FOR KIDS BY VICTIONARY 2
Viction:ary | 2003

2 BOOK TATTOOICONS BY VICTIONARY 3
Viction:ary | 2004
Complete with iconic design temporary tattoos.

3 IDN MY FAVORITE CONFERENCE VALUE PACK
IdN | 2004

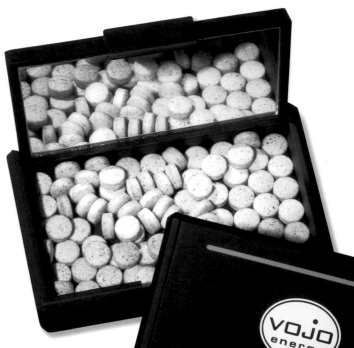

VOJO energy

PEPPERMINT

SUGAR FREE • GUARANA • VITAMIN B-12
net wt. 0.29 oz (8.25g)

VOJO energy

CITRUS

SUGAR FREE • GUARANA • VITAMIN C
net wt. 0.29 oz (8.25g)

VOJO ENERGY | CORONA DEL MAR
VOJO ENERGY BOXES
Joco Brands | 2005

WAACS DESIGN & CONSULTANCY | ROTTERDAM
GSUS UNDERWEAR AND ACCESSORIES
Gsus | 2004

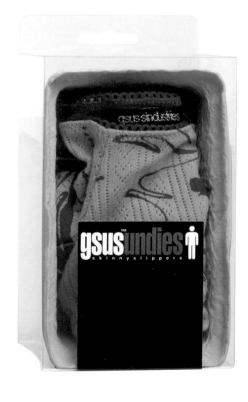

WARMRAIN | LONDON

1 CROISSANT BAG
Sketch | 2004
Wrapper, tablecloth and napkin in one.

2 INCENSE MATCHBOOK
Imli | 2005
Alternative to traditional matchbox for
non-smoking restaurant.

3 SCRUNCH PRESS RELEASE
Warmrain | 2005
Simplified the life of press agents by
pre-scrunching up their release.

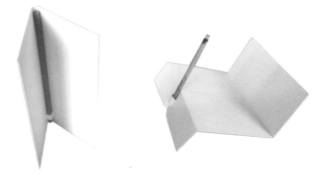

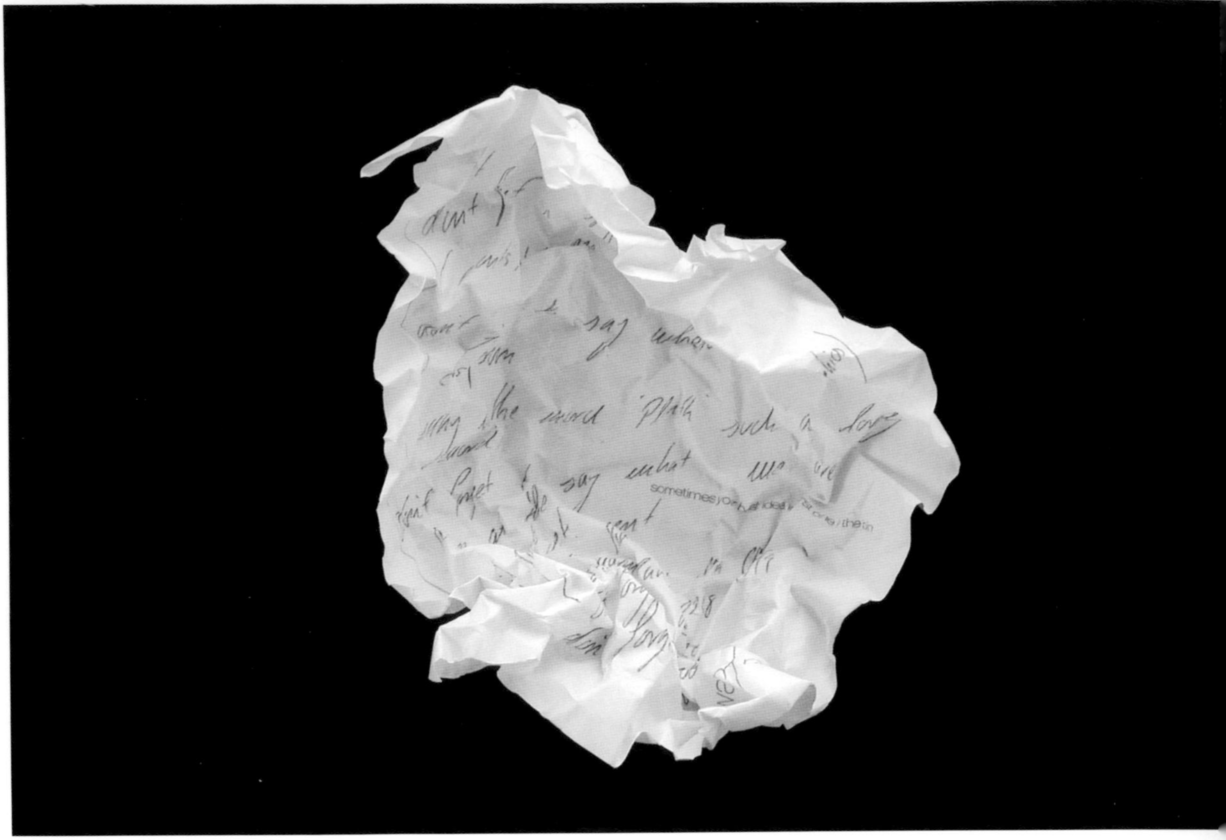

dont forget to say who we are
dont forget to say what we do
(events, ... marketing campaigns + graphics)

dont forget to say where Warm Rain
comes from

Why is the word "Plath" such a lovely
word?

dont forget to say what we are
doing at the moment

sometimes your best idea is the first one in the tin

dont forget.

dont forget to say that they can call

Jah Tairan Bell @ Warm Rain on 0208 980 14

or Linji Deakin @ Surgery on 0207 399

dont forget to say hello

dont forget to say goodbye

warm rain

BOSS
HUGO BOSS

SKIN
REFRESHING face wash
TONIFIANT nettoyant visage

150 ml e 5.0 FL

BOSS
HUGO BOSS

SKIN
INSTANT moisture gel
INSTANTANÉ gel hydratant

SKIN
REFRESHING face wash
TONIFIANT nettoyant visage

BOSS
HUGO BOSS

WEBB SCARLETT DEVLAM | LONDON

1 BOSS SKIN
  Procter & Gamble | 2005

2 FAIRY ACTIVE FOAM
  Procter & Gamble | 2006

3 FEEDING BOTTLE LOVABLE
  Webb Scarlett deVlam | 2005

FINGER RECESS

TWIST LOCK

GRIP DETAILS

"Give the Lady what she wants"

PARIS PERFUMES

Marshall Field's

3 stores become

(Text from the standing book, largely illegible:)

The start of a new millennium seemed a most appropriate time to celebrate the uniting of three great department stores under one name. In 2001, Dayton's and Hudson's joined under the Marshall Field's banner to create a better shopping experience for the guests we've been proud to serve throughout the 19th and 20th centuries and into the 21st century. **DAYTON'S.** Minneapolis-based Dayton's was among the nation's largest department stores for nearly a century. Founded in 1902 by George Draper Dayton, the store became synonymous with quality merchandise, superior fashion leadership and community involvement. Before changing its name to Marshall Field's, Dayton's stores numbered 19 in the Midwest. **J.L. HUDSON COMPANY.** For more than a century, the J.L. Hudson Company was a dominant force in Midwest retailing, with a strong reputation for fashion leadership and commitment to community involvement. Known as J.L. Hudson Company by most, The Dayton Company and J.L. Hudson became Dayton Hudson Corporation, with 21 Michigan stores now under the MARSHALL FIELD'S banner. The May Department Stores Company. Now, under the name of the respected Marshall Field's, department stores are located in Illinois, Indiana, Michigan, Minnesota, North Dakota, South Dakota and in Texas.

COMMUNITY GIVING. The Marshall Field's family of stores has a rich history of contributing to a variety of worthy causes and nonprofit organizations including support for the arts through our Marshall Field's Gives.

The Best

The Shop Heard Around the World

From its beginnings in downtown Chicago in 1852, Marshall Field's has earned a reputation of excellence through its landmark achievements, making it one of the premier department stores in the United States. Always a leader and innovator, Marshall Field's was the first department store to establish a European buying office, which was located in Manchester, England. It was the first to open a dining room restaurant and the first to offer a bridal registry. In addition, the store has established many lines of exclusive private-label merchandise, including our world-famous Frango® chocolates, as well as departments devoted to exquisite couture fashions, silver and jewelry.

THE LEGACY. Marshall Field himself is a great American success story. Starting out as a retail clerk, he became the pioneer of one of the most famous and recognized retail establishments in the world. He was also a major influence on how Chicago became the world-class city it is today. His legacy is still evident in places like the Art Institute of Chicago, The Field Museum and University of Chicago.

XAVIER DE BOLÒS, OCTAVI ROIG | BARCELONA
SPARE BULB KIT FOR VOLKSWAGEN ESPAÑA
Manipulados Karpak | 2005

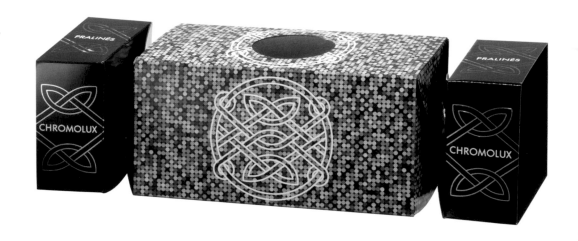

ZINNOBERGRUEN | DUSSELDORF
BONBONNIÈRES
M-real Zanders | 2005

Airside
24 Cross Street
London N1 2BG, UK
P +44 20 7354 9912
F +44 20 7354 5529
studio@airside.co.uk
www.airside.co.uk
Music Packaging
Photos © Airside

Alloy
1 Hurlands Business Centre
Farnham, Surrey GU9 9JE, UK
P +44 1252 712000
F +44 1252 712111
info@thealloy.com
www.thealloy.com
Cosmetic Bottles Original Source
Photos © Alloy

Amen
400 boul. de Maisonneuve O., bureau 700
Montréal, Québec H3A 1L4, Canada
P +1 514 847 0000
info@amencreation.com
www.amencreation.com
Shok
Photos © Amen

BAG.disseny
Placeta de Montcada 1-3
08003 Barcelona, Spain
P/F +34 933 194 962
info@bagdisseny.com
www.bagdisseny.com
T-Shirt Pack Clippack
Photos © BAG.disseny

Barskidesign
Hermannstrasse 15
60318 Frankfurt am Main, Germany
P +49 69 944190 70
F +49 69 944190 80
hello@barskidesign.com
www.barskidesign.com
Esso Ultra
Fürstenberg
Photos © Barskidesign

Beatriz Pérez, Clara Burguillo
Escola Massana
Dpt. Escola Empresa
Pere Duran
Hospital 56
08001 Barcelona, Spain
P +34 934 422 009
F +34 934 417 844
info@escolamassana.es
www.escolamassana.es
Gina Scooter
Photos © Escola Massana

Beyond Design
65 East Wacker Place, Suite 1610
Chicago, IL 60601, USA
P +1 312 201 6700
F +1 312 201 6701
info@beyonddesign.org
www.beyonddesign.org
Paintbuddy
Photos © Beyond Design

Big-Game
11 rue du Nord
11004 Lausanne, Switzerland
P +41 76 492 89 27
contact@big-game.ch
www.big-game.ch
Box
Photos © Millo Keller

Bloom
25 The Village, 101 Amies Street
London SW11 2JW, UK
P +44 20 7924 4533
F +44 20 7924 4553
debbie@bloom-design.com
www.bloom-design.com
23 Mixer
Photos © Bloom

Brandes en Meurs Industrial Design
Kerkstraat 19 C
3581 RA Utrecht, The Netherlands
P +31 30 231 02 06
info@brandesenmeurs.nl
www.brandesenmeurs.nl
Dremel Tool Kit
Skil Drill Gun
Photos © Brandes en Meurs

Capsule
10 South Fifth Street, Suite 645
Minneapolis, MN 55402, USA
P +1 612 341 4525
F +1 612 341 4577
info@capsule.us
www.capsule.us
Schroeder Milk
Photos © Capsule

Caracas
76 boulevard du 11 Novembre
69625 Lyon / Villeurbanne Cedex, France
P +33 4 78 68 77 87
F +33 4 78 68 77 88
caracas@caracas.fr
www.caracas.fr
Scissors Tattoo Package
Photos © Caracas

Catalina Hermida, Elise Lammer
Escola Massana
Dpt. Escola Empresa
Pere Duran
Hospital 56
08001 Barcelona, Spain
P +34 934 422 009
F +34 934 417 844
info@escolamassana.es
www.escolamassana.es
Adventure First Aid Kit
Photos © Escola Massana

Catalyst Design Group
252 Church Street Richmond
Melbourne, VIC 3121, Australia
P +61 3 9428 6352
F +61 3 9428 6897
info@catalyst.net.au
www.catalyst.net.au
Donut Tape Dispenser
Photos © Catalyst Design Group

Citrus
49 Cromwell Road, Great Glen
Leicester LE8 9GU, UK
P +44 870 124 8787
F +44 870 124 8742
us@citrus.co.uk
www.citrus.co.uk
Monotype Imaging Catalogue
Photos © Citrus

Cocktails by Jenn
P +1 646 218 6022
www.cocktailsbyjenn.com
Bottles and 4-Pack
Photos © Cocktails by Jenn

Curiosity
2-13-16 Tomigaya, Shibuya-ku
Tokyo 151-0063, Japan
P +81 03 5452 0095
F +81 03 5454 9691
info@curiosity.jp
www.curiosity.jp
Equilir Cosmetics
Parfum Curiosity
Photos © Masayuki Hayashi

Daniel Racamier
BP 14
74371 Pringy Cedex, France
P +33 4 50 27 26 85
www.maped.com
Box Scissors Créa Cut
FlexBox Color'Peps
Protect Box Color'Peps
Rubber Zenoa
Photos © Maped

DCA Design International
19 Church Street
Warwick CV34 4AB, UK
P +44 1926 499461
F +44 1926 401134
info@dca-design.com
www.dca-design.com
Célébrez Bottle
Drink Maintain Package
E Milk Bottle
Fruit Blast
Reward Vial
Photos © DCA Design International

Dew Gibbons
49 Tabernacle Street
London EC2A 4AA, UK
P +44 20 7689 8999
F +44 20 7689 9377
itsgreat@dewgibbons.com
www.dewgibbons.com
De Beers Jewelry Package (with Sebastian Bergne)
Photos © Dew Gibbons, Sebastian Bergne
The Body Shop Perfume Line
Photos © Dew Gibbons

Dotstation
Casanova 57, 3r 1a
08011 Barcelona, Spain
P +34 932 901 685
F +34 932 892 270
web@dotstation.es
www.dotstation.es
Sheer Cronoaging Range
Photos © Dotstation

Empire Creative Group/Gareth Dotchin
19 Budd Street
Collingwood, VIC 3066, Australia
P +61 03 9419 0061
F +61 03 9419 9144
gareth@empirecg.com.au
www.empirecg.com.au
Simply Green Tomatoes
Photos © Gareth Dotchin

Estudio Mariscal
Pellaires 30-38
08019 Barcelona, Spain
P +34 933 036 940
F +34 932 662 244
eva@mariscal.com
www.mariscal.com
CD Cover Lágrimas Negras
Photos © Estudio Mariscal

F Maurer
Rechte Bahngasse 40
1030 Vienna, Austria
P +43 1 512 10 30
F +43 1 512 10 40
design@fmaurer.com
www.fmaurer.com
Cosmetic Bottle
Photos © Franz Helmreich, Michael Zechany

Form
47 Tabernacle Street
London EC2A 4AA, UK
P +44 20 7014 1430
F +44 20 7014 1431
tom@form.uk.com
www.form.uk.com
Shelf Life Book Packaging
Photos © Form

376

Form Us With Love
Norra vägen 40
39235 Kalmar, Sweden
P +46 480 447375
petrus@formuswithlove.se
www.formuswithlove.se
Bendable Interior Objects
Photos © Form Us With Love

Freitag
Postfach
CH-8031 Zurich, Switzerland
P +41 43 210 33 33
drive-in@freitag.ch
www.freitag.ch
F69-Calcio
FTV Box Package Recycling
Twin Peaks
Photos © Freitag

FriendsConnexion
Hufelandgasse 1
1120 Vienna, Austria
P +43 1 547 15 33 0
F +43 1 547 15 33 34
team@friendsconnexion.com
www.friendsconnexion.com
Kitzbüheler Horn Chocolate Packaging
Photos © Mayr-Melnhof Packaging Austria

**Fuse Project / Yves Behar, Johan Liden,
Geoffrey Petrizzi**
528 Folsom Street
San Francisco, CA 94105, USA
P +1 415 908 1492
F +1 415 908 1491
info@fuseproject.com
www.fuseproject.com
Perfume 09
Photos © Robert Schlatter, Marcus Hanschen

Gateway Arts
810 Lawrence Drive, Suite 220
Thousand Oaks, CA 91320, USA
P +1 805 480 1140
F +1 805 480 1150
www.gatewayarts.com
Promotion Box
Photos © Gateway Arts

Gerard Moliné for Azuamoline.com
Rambla del Prat 8, 2n 2a
08012 Barcelona, Spain
P/F +34 932 182 914
gerardmoline@gmail.com
www.gerardmoline.com
www.azuamoline.com
Urna Bios
Photos © Gerard Moliné

Gilles Cenazandotti for Sartoria Comunicazione
6 rue Eugene Berthoud
93400 Saint Ouen, France
P +33 1 40 12 39 43
F +33 1 40 11 54 97
Limited Edition Defumo DVD Package
Photos © Defumo

Global Protection
12 Channel Street
Boston, MA 02210, USA
P +1 617 946 2800
F +1 617 946 3246
info@globalprotection.com
www.globalprotection.com
One Condoms
Photos © Global Protection

Groovisions
1-11-10 Naka-cho Meguro-ku
Tokyo 153-0065, Japan
P +81 03 5723 6558
F +81 03 5723 6356
grv@groovisions.com
www.groovisions.com
100% Chocolate Cafe Packaging
Photos © Groovisions

Harry Allen & Associates
207 Avenue A
New York, NY 10009, USA
P +1 212 529 7239
F +1 212 529 7982
office@harryallendesign.com
www.harryallendesign.com
Essentials Compact
Ukuru Lip Pigment
Photos © Harry Allen & Associates

Icon Development Group
18620 Crenshaw Blvd.
Torrance, CA 90504, USA
P +1 310 769 1200
F +1 310 769 0400
info@iconpackaging.com
www.iconpackaging.com
Tresdon Wine Rack
Photos © Icon Development Group

IDEO
White Bear Yard
144a Clerkenwell Road
London EC1R 5DF, UK
P +44 20 7713 2600
F +44 20 7713 2601
feedback@ideo.com
www.ideo.com
Natureworks "Pla" Bio-Plastic Concepts

Jouer Cosmetics
9465 Wilshire Blvd., Suite 400
Beverly Hills, CA 90212, USA
P +1 310 601 2419
info@jouercosmetics.com
www.jouercosmetics.com
Jouer Compact
Photos © Jouer Cosmetics

Karim Rashid
357 West 17th Street
New York, NY 10011, USA
P +1 212 929 8657
F +1 212 929 0247
office@karimrashid.com
www.karimrashid.com
Echo by Davidoff
Issey Miyake's Father's Day Kit
Photos © Karim Rashid

Kejadonia Design & Communicatie
PO Box 75076
1117 ZP Schiphol-Oost, The Netherlands
P +31 20 671 51 41
F +31 20 676 13 43
rtroost@kejadonia.nl
www.kejadonia.nl
Royal Club Bottles
Photos © Kejadonia Design & Communicatie

Kinetic Singapore
2 Leng Kee Rd, 04-03A, Thye Hong Ctr
159086 Singapore, Singapore
P +65 647 59 377
F +65 647 25 440
info@kinetic.com.sg
www.kinetic.com.sg
The Observatory CD Cover
Photos © Kinetic Singapore

Kokokumaru
507 Uni Higashiumeda, 7-2 Minamiogimachi Kita-ku
Osaka 530-0052, Japan
P +81 6 6314 0881
F +81 6 6314 0806
y-5590@ra2.so-net.ne.jp
www.kokokumaru.com
Dust Book
Kekkai Book
RoboCup 2005 Osaka
Photos © Kokokumaru

Landor Associates
Klamath House
18 Clerkenwell Green
London EC1R 0QE, UK
P +44 20 7880 8394
F +44 20 7880 8001
more_info@landor.com
www.landor.com
Evian Origine
Photos © Landor Associates

Laura Millán
Unió 32, pral. 2
08001 Barcelona, Spain
P +34 655 407 329
pitijopo@gmail.com
Cosmetic Packaging Vijuvi
Yogoy
Photos © Dustan Lee Shepard, Diethild Meier

Laura Nogaledo, Rut Rovira
Escola Massana
Dpt. Escola Empresa
Pere Duran
Hospital 56
08001 Barcelona, Spain
P +34 934 422 009
F +34 934 417 844
info@escolamassana.es
www.escolamassana.es
Galileo Galilei Sector
Photos © Escola Massana

Liston + Platon
6/224 Commonwealth Street
Surry Hills NSW 2010, Australia
P +61 2 9211 4342
F +61 2 9475 0283
info@listonplaton.com.au
www.listonplaton.com.au
Kevin Murphy Hair Care Products
Photos © Liston + Platon

LondonBerlin
BerlinLondon ltd
Markus Hohl
10a Brooklands Park, London se3 9bl, UK
P +44 770 277 5269
F +44 208 318 1503
info@berlinlondon.com

LondonBerlin gbr
Susanne Ewert
Crellestrasse 19-20, 10827 Berlin, Germany
P +49 30 787 04891
F +49 30 787 14939
ewert@londonberlin.de
www.londonberlin.de
Transport, Style and Chrome Box for Earphone Sport

Marc Atlan Design
434 Carroll Canal
Venice, CA 90291, USA
P +1 310 306 8148
F +1 310 306 8348
info@marcatlan.com
www.marcatlan.com
Comme des Garçons Fragrances Collection
Photos © Marc Atlan

Mathieu Lehanneur
9-11 rue du Roule
75001 Paris, France
P +33 8 70 39 24 39
F +33 1 40 26 24 39
m@mathieulehanneur.com
www.mathieulehanneur.com
Familles-Families
Photos © Studio spap shot
Therapeutic Objects
Photos © Véronique Huyghe, Courtesy MoMA, New York

Mayr-Melnhof Karton AG
Stephan Sweerts-Sporck
Brahmsplatz 6
1041 Vienna, Austria
P +43 1 501 36 91180
F +43 1 501 36 91195
www.mayr-melnhof.com
Kitzbüheler Horn Chocolate Packaging
Photos © Mayr-Melnhof Karton

Metaphase Design Group
2 South Hanley Road
St. Louis, MO 63105, USA
P +1 212 572 6263
barbara@spier-associates.com
www.metaphase.com
Drink'n Crunch
Photos © Tony Cenicola

Mihoko Hachiuma for Office M
5-25-6-1 Tohzu Kochi-shi
Kochi 781-0114, Japan
creer@mocha.ocn.ne.jp
"Imo Kempi" Packaging
Photos © Mihoko Hachiuma, Office M

Milkxhake
3/F, B, Lam Shan Building, 113-119 Belcher's Street
Kennedy Town, Hong Kong, China
P +852 6339 9740
javin@milkxhake.org
www.milkxhake.org
Motclub 903
Photos © Milkxhake

Morera Design
Pellaires 30-38
08019 Barcelona, Spain
P +34 933 036 990
F +34 932 660 415
morera@moreradesign.com
www.moreradesign.com
VV Man
VV Woman
Photos © Morera Design

No Picnic
Ljusslingan 1
SE 120 31 Stockholm, Sweden
P +46 8 55696550
F +46 8 6434410
info@nopicnic.se
www.nopicnic.se
Ankle and Elbow Rehband Supports
Photos © Anna-Lena Ahlström
Space Food Packaging
Photos © Camilo Matiz
Sport Underwear Packaging
Photos © Anna-Lena Ahlström

Octavi Roig
Amigó 42, àtic
08021 Barcelona, Spain
P +34 696 096 356
octaviroig@yahoo.com
Spare Bulb Kit for Volkswagen España
(with Xavier de Bolòs)
Photos © Xavier de Bolòs

Olivier Marrache for Designum Tremens
14 rue Maurice Fonvieille
31000 Toulouse, France
P/F +33 5 61 21 20 58
Glass
Photos © Olivier Marrache

Papermint Design
Strandpromenaden 27
2100 Copenhagen, Denmark
P +45 39 27 60 11
F +45 39 27 60 33
info@papermint.dk
www.papermint.dk
The Beautiful Swan
Photos © Papermint Design

Parker Williams
1st Floor, Voysey House, Barley Mow Passage
London W4 4PT, UK
P +44 20 8995 6411
www.parkerwilliams.co.uk
Disney Dough
Photos © Parker Williams

Pep Torres
Gloria 7, entresòl 2a
08902 Hospitalet de Llobregat, Spain
P +34 933 327 930
info@stereo-noise.com
www.stereo-noise.com
#32 Tomato & #53 Carrot
Eggminence
Filmitos
Photos © Figueroa & Stallard

Pure Equator
The Old School House, The Heritage Center
High Pavement, The Lace Market
Nottingham NG1 1HN, UK
P +44 115 947 6444
david.rogers@pure-equator.com
www.pure-equator.com
Label M Haircare Line
Photos © Pure Equator

Radi Designers
89, rue de Turenne
75003 Paris, France
P +33 1 42 71 29 57
F +33 1 42 71 29 62
ageslin@radidesigners.com
www.radidesigners.com
Marlboro Matches
Photos © Radi Designers

RDYA
Avda. del Libertador 6570, 3°
C1428ARV Buenos Aires, Argentina
P/F +54 11 4115 1500
info@rdya.com
www.rdya.com
RDYA Promotional Packaging
Vaja
Photos © RDYA

Ricardo Manrique, Ander Solano
Escola Massana
Dpt. Escola Empresa
Pere Duran
Hospital 56
08001 Barcelona, Spain
P +34 934 422 009
F +34 934 417 844
info@escolamassana.es
www.escolamassana.es
Packaging for Cactus
Photos © Escola Massana

Ross Lovegrove
21 Powis Mews
London W11 1JN, UK
P +44 20 7229 7104
F +44 20 7229 7032
anka@rosslovegrove.com
www.rosslovegrove.com
Ty Nant Bottle
Photos © John Ross, Ty Nant

Sagmeister
222 West 14 Street, Suite 15 A
New York, NY 10011, USA
P +1 212 647 1789
F +1 212 647 1788
info@sagmeister.com
www.sagmeister.com
Skeleton Key CD
The Vanity Allegory
Photos © Sagmeister

Saguez and Partners
14 rue Palouzié
93400 Saint-Ouen, France
P +33 1 41 66 64 00
m.ledreau@saguez-and-partners.com
www.saguez-and-partners.com
Lafayette Maison Range
Photos © Saguez and Partners

Sandstrom Design
808 SW Third, 610
Portland OR 97204, USA
P +1 503 248 9466
F +1 503 227 5035
rick@sandstromdesign.com
www.sandstromdesign.com
Castor & Pollux Range of Products
gDiapers Packaging
Photos © Sandstrom Design

Sebastian Bergne
Via Castiglione 90
40124 Bologna, Italy
P +39 051 19982256
mail@sebastianbergne.com
www.sebastianbergne.com
De Beers Jewelry Package (with Dew Gibbons)
Photos © Dew Gibbons, Sebastian Bergne

Sergio Calatroni Art Room
Corso di Porta Nuova, 46/b
20121 Milan, Italy
P +39 02 655 581 6
F +39 02 454 740 27
info@sergiocalatroni.com
www.sergiocalatroni.com
Stephane Marais Cosmetics
Photos © Sergio Calatroni Art Room

Strichpunkt
Schönleinstrasse 8a
70184 Stuttgart, Germany
P +49 711 620327 0
F +49 711 620327 10
info@strichpunkt-design.de
www.strichpunkt-design.de
DTP Typometer
Photos © Strichpunkt

Sweden Graphics
Blekingegatan 46
SE 116 64 Stockholm, Sweden
P +46 8 6520066
F +46 8 6520033
hello@swedengraphics.com
www.swedengraphics.com
Bliw Soap
Photos © Sweden Graphics

Tank Tromsø
Storgata 36, Postboks 751
9258 Tromsø, Norway
P +47 77 69 90 26
ottem@tank.no
www.tank.no
SMRPRTY Beer Bottle
Photos © Tank Tromsø

The Partners
Albion Courtyard, Greenhill Rents, Smithfield
London EC1M 6PQ, UK
P +44 7608 0051
liz@thepartners.co.uk
www.thepartners.co.uk
Stanley Honey
Stella McCartney Bags
Photos © The Partners

Turnstyle
2219 NW Market Street
Seattle, WA 98107, USA
P +1 206 297 7350
F +1 206 297 7390
info@turnstylestudio.com
www.turnstyle-inc.com
Dry Soda Bottles
Teague Mailer
Photos © Turnstyle

Viction:ary
Unit 2202, 22nd Floor, Kingsfield Centre
18-20 Shell Street, North Point, Hong Kong, China
P +852 2877 0281
F +852 2887 7630
we@victionary.com
www.victionary.com
Book Design for Kids by Victionary 2
Book Tattooicons by Victionary 3
IdN My Favorite Conference Value Pack
Photos © Viction:ary

Vojo Energy
2101 East Coast Hwy, Suite 250
Corona del Mar, CA 92625, USA
P +1 877 566 4687 / +1 949 760 4445
F +1 310 388 5647
media@vojoenergy.com
www.vojoenergy.com
Vojo Energy Boxes
Photos © Joco Brands

Volker Schumann & Karel Golta for Solutions
Solutions
Sternstrasse 117
20357 Hamburg, Germany
P +49 40 432006 67
F +49 40 432006 75
info@solutions.de
www.solutions.de
Compo Fertilizer Range
Photos © Solutions

Waacs Design & Consultancy
Hennekijnstraat 37-b
3012 EB Rotterdam, The Netherlands
P +31 10 412 69 99
F +31 10 412 86 57
more@waacs.com
www.waacs.com
GSUS Underwear and Accessories
Photos © Waacs Design & Consultancy

Warmrain
67 Vyner Street, Bethnal Green
London E2 9DQ, UK
P +44 20 8980 1984
F +44 20 8980 1986
studio@warmrain.co.uk
www.warmrain.co.uk
Croissant Bag
Incense Matchbook
Scrunch Press Release
Photos © Warmrain

Webb Scarlett deVlam
12 Junction Mews
London W2 1PN, UK
P +44 20 7706 8076
F +44 20 7706 8086
ian.webb@wsdv.com
www.wsdv.com
Boss Skin
Fairy Active Foam
Feeding Bottle Lovable
Photos © Webb Scarlett deVlam

Wink
126 North 3rd Street, No. 100
Minneapolis, MN 55401, USA
P +1 612 455 2642
F +1 612 455 2645
info@wink-mpls.com
www.wink-mpls.com
Jewelry Accessory Kit
Photos © Wink

Xavier de Bolòs
Buenos Aires 4, 5° 2ª
08029 Barcelona, Spain
P/F +34 933 226 504
debolos@coac.net
Spare Bulb Kit for Volkswagen España
(with Octavi Roig)
Photos © Xavier de Bolòs

Zinnobergruen
Fürstenwall 79
40217 Düsseldorf, Germany
P +49 211 994594 94
F +49 211 994594 99
office@zinnobergruen.de
www.zinnobergruen.de
Bonbonnières
Photos © Zinnobergruen

© 2008 daab
cologne london new york

published and distributed worldwide by
daab gmbh
friesenstr. 50
d - 50670 köln

p + 49 - 221 - 913 927 0
f + 49 - 221 - 913 927 20

mail@daab-online.com
www.daab-online.com

publisher ralf daab
rdaab@daab-online.com

creative director feyyaz
mail@feyyaz.com

editorial project by loft publications
© 2008 loft publications

editor and text lou andrea savoir
research àgata losantos, àlex sánchez and catherine collin

layout loft publications
english translation bridget vranckx
german translation simone schleifer
spanish translation julio fajardo
italian translation alessandro orsi

front cover © warmrain

printed in italy
www.zanardi.it

isbn 978-3-937718-59-0